LYFE'S LYRICS
LIFE LESSONS TO HELP YOUNG MEN TRANSITION INTO MANHOOD

Zane Edwards

LYFE'S LYRICS

Written by: Zane Edwards

A Message to the Reader

These lyrics of wisdom allow me the privilege to share with the people who read this book, the gift the Lord has given me. I have worked all my life trying to be the best man I can be. Little did I know, this meant being the man the Lord would have me to be. Any self-made man will find it hard to be prepared for life's path. As a reader of this book, you will see I have a different style of writing. I call it, *a play on words* – a combination of words and parables to feed the spiritual mind. Each person who reads my lyrics will be able to identify with what is relative to them. I would like to say to all the young men and women: ***Your role in life is an important one.*** This book will bring that out, for all to see. My purpose in releasing this book is to help as many people as possible understand *who they are in their own minds*, in effort to assist them as they travel their life's path. One of many...

"To yourself, first be true. Then your path in life will become clear to you."

TABLE OF CONTENTS

Change

Insight

The Heart

TABLE OF CONTENTS

Wisdom

Sneak Preview of *Self Threat*

CHANGE

*"For I am Jehovah; I do not **change**."*
–Malachi 3:6

Inspiration Statement: Each new day is a fresh start.

Today Is A New Day

Today is a new day, what more can I say
It's our turn, and will you learn

Avoid the big lie, It's important that you try
In your heart, you know the reason why

We must make this change before we can move on
Why have we waited so long to learn to be strong?

We always want to blame someone else
Yet and still we can only blame ourselves

If the truth is to be told, we can feel it in our soul
The desire of the heart is what sets us apart

Always choose good before you choose bad,
Otherwise, you will wish you never had

Today is a new day, let's try a different way
The way we tried last is now in our past

We cannot continue to be mean
With all the things in our past we have seen

Do you know whether you want better?
To say yes is to get rid of stress

It doesn't matter whether you are a woman or a man
In life, we all must take a stand

Inspiration Statement: Wisdom in the combination of words.

A Play On Words

No matter what in the past you have heard
The key to understanding is a play on words

Something can be said in many ways
To follow a person, talking seems hard to do nowadays

Some people may be from the state of Maine
Others may speak with a southern slang

It's up to each of us how our words are used
The task is not to leave a person confused

Words can describe good
Or something bad, happy or sad

A play on words at times
Depends on what a person wants to hear
It's important that they know we are sincere

Filthy communication, many times, is used without hesitation
It is not important if the words you use are dirty or clean
As long as a person knows what you mean

You may speak soft or even loud
Only you know what it takes for your crowd

Don't worry and have no doubt
You will be understood
As long as you know what you're talking about

To express words is how we learn
Otherwise, we may not know which way to turn

Trouble comes when we speak – knowing we are mad
The outcome normally turns out bad

Choose your words with this in mind
To properly express is to be kind

You may be talking about love or sex
The key is to know what words to use next

Some words you hear, you may love or hate
The meaning of the words is what keeps us straight

The use of words is a powerful tool
A good example is the words Jesus used

Wisdom, knowledge, and understanding
Comes when we are blessed with insight
A combination of words we receive with true delight

Open your eyes and your ears
To understand as it appears

To some, wisdom may seem to hide
To others, it's a matter of swallowing our pride

The true play on words start and stops with you
As we go through each day
We never know the words we are going to say

Remember for each person you meet
Understanding is what we all should seek

Express yourself and don't leave it up to no one else
After all, no matter what in life you may do
No one can stand at the judgment bar for you

Choose your words and always try to be wise

Never use words you have to disguise
It's like speaking nothing but lies

As you seek wisdom, always get understanding
For life is so demanding

You were little and now you say you are grown
But ask yourself…can you really stand on your own?

A play on words is to have meaning in what you have to say
It's very important to be understood every day

A Play On Words

Inspiration Statement: Unconditional love.

Compassion

Compassion is from a pure heart
For each person that holds it, it is a work of art
To reveal, sometimes we have to hold back tears
Do you have it? Have you noticed it over the years?
Can you recognize it as it appears?
Compassion started with Jehovah…You can feel it all over
It can happen at any time throughout Mankind
It can save a life no matter what the price
To have compassion is to avoid telling a lie
It allows you to know the reasons why
With compassion, it takes away hate – you cannot participate
To desire a heart of compassion is never too late
It's in you, even on this date
No matter what people do to you
Compassion will see you through
Compassion comes from love, given by the Lord above
He has it for me and you
He is always there to see us through
Times today in life have gotten so very hard
From Jesus, compassion is no charge
People will say and do what they will
Compassion is to say, "Peace, be still."
This helps how you feel
Compassion applies in life every day
To have it, makes a way out of no way
Compassion has only one rule: You must have love as your tool
In people, you will see the good, the bad, and the ugly
This is why you must continue to study
No one is above the law
Do you really know what Jesus saw?
The Father, Son, Holy Ghost
Compassion is from our heavenly host
You can see compassion every direction you turn
This is something we all must learn

Inspiration Statement: To be aware at all times, as we look through the window of our eyes.

Focus

In our minds, we need to be focused at all times
It's key to where we should be
We must focus and be direct
Have the desire of what to do next
A focus of sight allows you to do what's right
Focus on the past is to know what was last
To focus on the here and now allows us to figure out how
To focus on the future is to make plans, then take a stand
Focus is true insight, an awareness of what is just and right
A focus of mind has aim, to lose it will result in pain
Stay focused, this will not allow you to be blamed
A focused mind saves time, stay alert so you don't get hurt
Focus on peace, the chaos will cease
A focused mind is to be blessed
It will allow you to control the flesh
Focus on that which is true, make it a part of you
Focus every day as you will, focus until your heart is filled
Focus can bring you joy, only if you don't be coy
Stay focused and be no one's fool
To be manipulated as their tool
Focus with good purpose and good intent
Focus and let the world know you are God-sent
Focus on Jesus above and the world will see pure love
Stay focused no matter where you may be
Your Lord will always allow you to see
Jesus will not have you blind
Live as an example to Mankind
To be focused is your right, then you will never lose sight
Focus within, and you will see all the Lord would have you to be
Focus on the love in your heart, for this is where all things start
Focus

Inspiration Statement: Recognizing where we are in our path of life at this moment.

Here and now

Time allows us to understand how we got here now
Focus on yourself and no one else
Be sincere in your heart all must become clear
Here and now is a moment in time
As you follow your life's path line
Can you walk the path line of time? What will you find?
Will it be a peace of mind?
Will you decline if you have no sign?
Please don't fall behind, many people are blind
Some have lost track of time
Here and now, what do you feel inside?
Will your emotions hide? Will your arms open wide?
What will it be? Open your heart and let us see
There's plenty of work to do, to your heart be true
Out of the heart flows the issue of life
We are compelled to be nice
Can we make the sacrifice?
Choose to be wise and open your eyes
What will we gain? We can all avoid life's pain
Will you maintain and be sane?
We all must stay in our lane and success in life will be gained
Here and now is an important point we must learn
So we won't be burned and pass the point of no return
Can you outlast things of the past that required moving fast?
Here and now freezes time, it can be any time
As these words are said, time can be read
What will you be going through?
As these words come to you, will you be happy or sad?
Rejoice and be glad
Here and now, take a stand...life has many demands
Things are worthwhile when you have your first child
A boy, or even a girl, can brighten your world
Here and now, how did you get here?
Was it out of fear? Be of good cheer
At times the path in life seems like a dream

Things happen to us, unfair and mean
Stop, look, listen and pray
You will always find your way
Every day is the Lord's Day
Here and Now

Inspiration Statement: To be present and accounted for.

Roll call

Roll call pertains to us all
We must identify the things in our life, and not deny
We have to face the reasons why
To know the clue is to recognize the things for you
Roll call is to say you are present and accounted for
We cannot ignore
Can you pass the class, may I ask?
Well let's see as it is given to me
For the burdens we bear, we must always care...Are you aware?
It's easy to tell yourself a lie and never question why
So to hear the term roll call, that's not all
Chaos will have you bouncing off the walls
Are we ready to answer the call?
People eat for health and some for hardy
Some of us, all we want to do is party
Some hold a lot of hate, as many of us may state
It really doesn't carry much weight
The bottom line is to be kind and know when you are telling lies
Roll call, can you answer?
If you don't, it can act as cancer
When Jesus calls upon you, what will you do?
Do you even have a clue?
If you're like me, I didn't know where I would be
Do you have His love?
Then you will accept that which comes from above
If we hold a lot of pride, this means we have denied
Have you lied?
It's very hard to deal with the lust of the flesh
To begin telling you what's involved dealing with the rest
When you hear roll call, it's designed to alert us all
To caution you so you won't fall
Stay alert to save yourself from anguish and hurt
Stay in the Word, so it's not something you haven't heard
To be ready is to be in the word steadily
That which is spirit is spirit, that which is flesh is flesh

This helps you to overcome many tests
We see many things we think we want
We really don't know whether we do or don't
Remember this, no matter what road you choose...
You will always stand a chance to lose
Now many of us are singing the blues
Lust of the flesh is nothing more than a major test
The spirit of man is the key
It allows us to be all we can be
Our thoughts, Jesus always knows
Each and every day, He beholds

Inspiration Statement: The Lord's way, or my way?

Righteousness vs. Selfishness

Should we walk in the way that's right?
Should we do what we want out of spite?
To do what is right is so very hard
To do it is to set us apart
To all that reads this, far and near...
The things I say with this lyric
You may not want to hear
Yet, I must say it as the Lord puts it in my ear
As we walk through life, trying to be the best we can be
Many times, our journey is hard to see
Each day, we deal with many issues
Some days brings tears that requires tissues
In life, there's a line
Who said life was fair as we deal with mankind?
"Mankind", a name we all are a part of
The problems in life we struggle to get above
It's harder when we show no love
Many of us throw rocks and hide our hands
Well, it's time we take a stand
Is there guilt in many of you?
Guilt is a role I have played, too
Everyone wants to be right and not be wrong
We never understood this until love is gone
"Am I..?" is the question we must ask ourselves
"Doing things for me or for someone else?"
Wisdom and health becomes very important as we age
At times, loved ones speak what's right
And we resort to rage
"I don't want to hear it."
"You don't tell me what to do."
The bottom line is that they are saying what is true
It's up to you and I to choose to listen or deny
Doing what's right doesn't make a holy roller
Advice isn't meant to be a controller
If you walk with feet burning with fire

———

Would you walk and have the desire?
There is a path we can walk that is cool
Just remember there are some rules
Righteousness will always be true to you
This is a very important clue
"I" and "me", is to speak of oneself
It doesn't allow space for no one else
To yourself be true
Then, the path will be clear to you

Inspiration Statement: Living wrong.

Sin

Sin, is a word for us to be shown where we belong
Not a sad song, it points out where we went wrong
We aren't doing right, it's because we have lost sight
It's important for us for to know
What it takes to stay in the light
At times, our focus is on the flesh
I am guilty as all the rest
That which is spirit is spirit
That which is flesh is flesh
When we know the difference
It's hard to do our best
Lust is the feeling of the heart
So strong, you should have control from the start
It is said, to live a life of sin
Is a game you cannot win
No one knows where in life I have been
As the story goes, only God knows where or when
As the lyricist and the writer,
Let me shed some light to make things brighter
When time begin, mankind quickly sinned
As time passed over the ages
It is known to man what sin wages
As you may have heard,
The term "sin" comes from God's Word
Yet, as we talked about our sin
Some of us are disturbed
Do you know if it is a verb?
To avoid sin, we must take time to think
The answers are written with pin and ink
Sin is like adding salt
It would never happen without our given thought
The battle has been fought
And the victory has been won
This was done by God's only begotten Son
In life, sin is a mess…it's not for play

We all have to find our way
Sin is something we all should know about
Yet, something we won't sing and shout
As we all do it, it's nothing to it
We have to pay a price, to make it through it
Jesus came to show us the way out of sin
Yet, many of us will be doing it until the very end

Inspiration Statement: Understanding what you feel in your spirit.

What Is It? Do you feel?

This lyric is for everyone who has a heart to feel
As we go through life, we must always keep it real
This day, this hour, you may wonder
Did your mother have a baby shower?

It's the little thoughts in life that can really teach thee
But we must be willing and able to see
To feel as you feel is to know the reasons why
We must also know the difference between the truth and a lie

Right now, many of us may feel the pressure of our jobs
To get past it is like going through life's door
Holding the knob

For some of us, life may seem a stretch
We are confused and don't know what to do next
Many have the desire to live life with glitz and glamour
Then others feel life has crushed them with a hammer

What's your story and what's your view?
Did your goals in life come true?
As we travel through life we seek peace
Do you know if it will be enough to teach?

For many of you may not have heard
In the past I have said, life can be a play on words
For every moment we have a bad thought
Remember you will always get caught

There is a price for us to pay if we desire to be that way
Love is a powerful word to use
Many of us will always seem to abuse

To be in love is a great way to feel
But only with someone who is real

Yes, you can find someone if that is your will
Just remember they must have more than sex appeal

The moral of this story I'm telling you
Is to get you to understand your life's view
What is this, you may ask?
How can you know what I have done in my life's path?

I am not judge, nor jury, I pray you won't be weary
To be upset is not to know what's coming next
Anger can devour you, pay attention to life's clues

We are in the bosom of fools, because we don't know the rules
Yes, rules, rules, those things are an important life tool
Some of you say I may speak in parables
To others, bits and pieces
Behold, this is what life teaches

You may say, "Mr. Writer, what you say is for the birds."
No, but Jesus will get the last words
Remember, I am nothing, and He has it all
For He is the one to make the judgment calls

INSIGHT

*"And those having **insight** will shine as brightly as the expanse of heaven..."*

–Daniel 12:3

Inspiration Statement: To understand life.

Do You Understand?

To understand life is so very hard
It's a difficult task from the start
Wisdom and knowledge isn't very clear
The desire in my heart to learn is sincere
My days as a child, I desired to be grown
Little did I know, I should have stayed home
We learned a little, and think we know a lot
We get among friends, then we are on the spot
We all desire to look good
But did you learn the things you should?
To understand, you must have insight
Receive knowledge with joy and not spite
You must be open to gain knowledge with truth
For a foolish man to understand,
Is like pulling a tooth
For knowledge, and the lack of,
Is to know your spirit starves
We all desire to be the best we can be
It's up to us to receive that which we can see
We think we know everything
But yet we know nothing
If we're honest with ourselves
We can learn something
To, understand must be a desire in you
For everyday, the sky is the color blue
Do not hold on to envy and strife
Yet, are you willing to pay the price?
I have understanding many will say
Then why has your life turned out this way?
For your bad things in life
There is no one else to blame
If you have understanding
Would things turn out the same?
Many of us, to our friends we want to impress
This only comes when we strive to be the best

The key to understanding comes as I say to you
Some, you may say, are not true
Do you have a better idea?
Please explain how you got here
If now, your future you cannot see
Then at this time, please listen to me
The key fact of life is to find our way
You are at the crossroads of life
Now, what do you say?
This way, that way…what will you do?
Now within you, can you choose?
To understand life comes from God
For each and every day, He is in charge
Jesus Christ came here to teach
Through Him, all wisdom can be reached
For those of us that hold stubbornness and pride
From you, true wisdom and knowledge will hide
For only a humble man can understand
For all others, feet are walking in sinking sand
In your heart to yourself, first be true
Then, you will allow Jesus to teach you
Now, to you it has been made plain
Now, as you go, your life will not be the same
From the stories of old, you may have heard
True wisdom and knowledge comes from the Word
"What word is this?" you may ask
For the answer is no great task
Here throughout the present time and the past
Through it all, it will last
The holy Bible, I say to you
Now, you have the true and just clue
Now, you hold the answer in your hand
As I said in the beginning, do you understand?

Inspiration Statement: To express *my* view of love.

Love

This is a subject many want to talk about
I guess it's my turn and we will see how it turns out
Love is of the heart, it has been from the very start
It is an emotion we all can share
If only we would dare
Love can save a person's life
Love can help us overcome strife
Love can be described in many ways
It can bring a peace of mind these days
To love is to hold that which is true
In our soul, that which sees us through
Love is the key to being nice
To show it is the ultimate price
Love covers a multitude of sin
Each of us knows what we hold within
Love is more than having sex
A moment in time when many
Don't care what is next
To love, we must be able to forgive
Harden not your heart is God's will
Love can, in life, be our guide
All we have to do is get rid of our pride
Love is the one that brought you home last night
Otherwise, we would fuss and fight
Love is a word that can go on and on
Love is the basis on which the world was born
Love in everyday life applies
Love is what keeps us from telling lies
To speak of love, many say, "What is this?"
Emotions and feelings with twist
This lyric of love was by request
As I write, I will pass the test
Love is what we feel, with special appeal
Later to find out we weren't keeping it real
Love of life is always nice

———

But some days, it's like rolling dice
To speak of love is so much on this earth
Without it, you know the world gets worse
We must love our brother and our sister
To break your heart, will hurt even quicker
Love is not a game people should play
Love is what keeps us each and everyday
To understand love
You must know it comes from God
Without Him, you will lose because of the odds

Inspiration Statement: To measure one's position in life.

Status of Life

Status of life, take time to say it twice
To some, it may be a new edition
It's more about life's position

When we think of people in our past, we try to remember
Where we have seen them last
Status of life, to some, things may not have been nice
Will it be a good report?
Maybe today you have to show up in court

Have you crossed the line? Did you abuse drugs or even wine?
Please tell the truth, I haven't seen you since our youth
On the news, was it me you thought you would see?
Status of life, are you willing to pay the price?

What will you have?
At times life flows
Like water pouring from a valve
I'm speaking of a faucet
You may be thinking of the opposite

Life at times moves at a fast pace
And we don't have time to waste
Status of life, at this time, can you afford a bowl of rice?

Are you like all the rest?
Do you measure status by your success?
Status of life no matter how much, you and I may try
Others always seem to lie

What's your will? How do you choose to live?
Handouts do you receive, or do you give out?

Status of life can be obtained many ways these days
It's up to you to see it through
Now what will you do?

When you focus, what do you see?
Do you know where you want to be?
What's your family tree?

Inspiration Statement: Tired of favoritism on the job.

The Good Ole Boy System

Writing this lyric, I will do with pride
So sit back and let's take a ride
Once this system starts to overcome it, is a work of art
To all far and near, please lend me your ear
For this system to be recognized,
We must be very wise
I'm writing this lyric to save time, so you won't be blind
As you go in the door as a worker, you want more
We desire to be the best we can be
At some companies, it's hard to believe what you may see
For all that read this purpose and intent
Just remember, writing this is a way to vent
You may say, "To vent is nothing but hot air."
On the other hand, it's to make others aware
The good ole boy system is by design
Until one day you cross that line
"What is this system?", you may ask
Well, just picture someone who always seems to get a free pass
Others will say they just kissed someone's ass
It's up to you to determine which is true
After all, your promotion and your raise is overdue
Pucker-up and blow a kiss into the wind
Who knows when this system began
Those that kissed will deny the reasons why
Others will say that it's just a lie
When we talk among people of things unjust
Make sure we are not jealous
If you earn it, that is fine
If you didn't, then you have crossed the line
Some of us have paid our dues and have a degree
You have a right to the success you seek

Inspiration Statement: Beware of bad people.

To Watch

As we go through life, many people will come against us a lot
To hold your peace, many times is all we got
We must sit back and watch, The Lord will fight our battles
As the bible has taught
When we travel the path of life, we must understand the rules
Anger is in the bosom of fools…this isn't a good tool to use
Every day, on our jobs, someone is trying to make it very hard
Life shows us evil is still at large
In our hearts, there are many things
We may say and want it our way
"Why did they do this to me?"
"They caught me blind and I couldn't see."
It's hard to hold your peace, to say the least
We must continue to be wise
Even when people are always telling lies
If we do what we have in mind, we will cross the line
At that time, the way out is very hard to find
Be slow to anger and keep this in mind
The lord teaches us to hold our peace and be still
The most important thing is His will

Inspiration Statement: Should life be this way?

What Should Be?

When we think of what should be
In our minds, it depends on what we see
As we go through life, we will make many sacrifices
What will you do? What is your life's clue?

To save time, be kind and seek a peace of mind
In life, every day we go through enough
Yet, you have to put up with today's stuff

You may say, "What, do you mean?"
"The things you say I haven't seen."
As you look through the windows of your eyes
Let your heart receive the truth
Then your path will become clear to you

Every day is a day to learn
The wisdom from it must be earned
Some may say I'm being a wise guy
No, I'm not denying the reasons why

Please hear my plea.
Pull from your family tree
The elders were here to teach thee

It doesn't matter what you have done in your past
It wasn't meant to last, it was just a major task
Something you had to do and make it through
This is when you know the Lord has blessed you

What should be is something we face every day and find a way
The best I can gather, this phrase, "What should be?"
Is an everyday subject matter

We all desire to be complete
You want to put things in place to have what we seek
What should be is what we need for life's path to flow
On the other hand, some of us never know

Life has a wide range and, at any time, things could change
Let's keep it plain and not insane
In life, there is plenty of wisdom to be gained

What should be?

Inspiration Statement: How to deal with coworkers.

Work

As I head to work, I wonder who calls me a jerk
It doesn't matter about the chit-chatter
Many people always have plenty to say
I am not going to let it ruin my day
As I arrive to my job alive
I'm going to keep things inside

There is one thing I am going to do
That is to tell you how I feel and keep my point of view
If you ask me reasons why
I would tell you it is better not to lie
In life, of all you may do, please keep it true
Behold, this is one of life's great clues

You may ask, what is all the fuss?
To live in life, to work is a must
To hold your peace on the job is very hard
The gossip can pull you apart
Sometimes, it's like ripping out your heart
Some days, I may be mad, and some people may be sad
The evildoer will be glad
If it's not right, sometimes you may want to fight
You may lose sight

The evildoer still finds delight
If we hold our peace, the chaos will cease
This isn't church, so stay alert, so you won't be hurt
When you walk in the door after turning the knob
Remember you and the evildoer is at odds

Inspiration Statement: Understanding desire.

Desire

We all have desire
Some of us wear it like clothing attire
Desire starts from the heart
Many of us are aware when it's taking part

Desire is sometimes considered lust
Yet, many of us do not know when we should trust
To trust your desire in many cases isn't a bad thing
For us, it depends on what it may bring

Desire can be an insight with great delight
I'm not the judge to say when is right
Desire can motivate, if only we participate
This is a state of mind, which dwells in all of Mankind

Desire can lead to many things
We must be willing to sprout wings
Desire can make us better lovers
This truly can please many sisters and brothers

Desire comes strong and sometimes weak
As for you, has it reached its peak?
Desire is a powerful word
For it's something we all deserve

Desire, what a wonderful feeling it can be
If only you were willing to see
Desire can be as a flaming fire
I hope and pray I'm not preaching to the choir

Desire is sometimes cold, but yet we must be bold
Take it by the hand, for in you make a stand
It can lead you to the Promised Land

Desire is no joke

This I must say to all you good folks
There is something I must add
Desire is good and also bad
Desire can help us reach our goals, even before we grow old
Desire in our heart, is what ignites any start

Desire can strengthen you to lead
This is something we all must believe
Desire inspires us to take a walk
For something that is more than just to talk

Do you have the desire to live or die?
Jesus has showed us why
Desire is our driver
The foundation of the survivor

Inspiration Statement: Having a lot to do.

To Do List

As I write this lyric To Do List, it comes with a twist
I'm speaking to everyone who has a lot to get done
This is for you and I to identify
Why we let many things to do get by
Your day may be full like water in a cup
Yet, there are no excuses – just results
What is it? We can't seem to get things done
We are not the only one
Well, let me tell you one good clue
Everything is up to you
We can save a lot of time
We must understand it takes a well, made-up mind
We will always have someone in our ear
Who has made it clear?
We can't hide behind our pride
Many people think, "Just let it ride."
For me, my wife has been a big help
This only has come because
I'm learning to be humble and willing to accept
Many days, our list seems to be very long
Some of us won't touch it, just leave it alone
To do list holds many twists
We can't make light of people who will do right
They will insist on completing their list
You don't have to ask, they will complete the task
For those of you whom this holds true
Maybe a "Thank you" is overdue
As for me, I hope my lists will soon be complete as I seek
Any less will seem like defeat
Men, women, boys and girls…please do not deny
The To Do List for you does apply

THE HEART

*"Above all the things that you guard, safeguard your **heart**, for out of it are the sources of life."*
–Proverbs 4:23

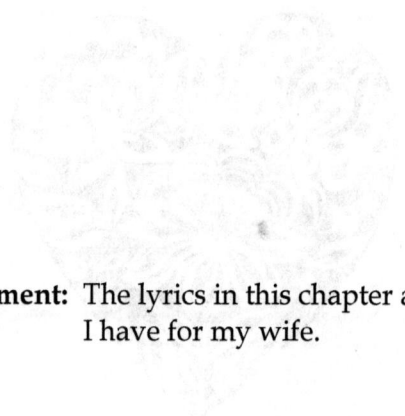

Inspiration Statement: The lyrics in this chapter are about the love
I have for my wife.

My Love

As I sit here in this chair, focused and very much aware
Life is like truth or dare
My love, I want you to know how much I care
My love, I say from my heart
I hope and pray this role is a permanent part
In life, many people seek their true love
We are blessed to be set far above
My love, you have brought me from darkness into the light
That is beautiful, bright, and right
My love, if I am ever asked, I will say
"To obtain true love is no easy task."
Many people don't know where they should be
Some are without love, blind and can't see
As for me, this love I have for you will never flee
You make my family tree
To go forward in the future, I am not blind
With you beside me, I can face Mankind

Inspiration Statement: When I first met my wife.

My Love, My Life, My Friend

I can't remember when
I didn't know how my lyric should begin
All I know is to tell this story that has unfold
We met when we were young
We had no clue our future had begun
She was with another guy she trust
I didn't have the right to be jealous
My life was going wild, as she was living a sheltered lifestyle
She was in love back then, and we weren't even friends
Life has many rules, and one thing is for sure
It's hard to follow clues
Long ago in my past, I saw her as she walked to her next class
Back then, of all the things I thought I might do
I truly can say I didn't have a clue
Now the story can be told
Because the story has now unfold
She asked her best friend who was I
The always smiling guy
I always kept my distance
Her best friend's name was Vincent
She then found out after all, Vincent and I played football
We were on the same team
Even though we didn't hang-out to be seen
As a senior, I had his respect
And the future, no one knew what was next
I finished high school and had to continue the path of life rules
Years later after that, I showed up where she was at
I had to go to the store,
And I saw her when I walked in the door
I had not seen her in a long while, so I greeted her with a smile
I said "Hello stranger, and how do you do?
Do you remember me or even have a clue?"
She smiled as I got in range
And her pretty eyes looked at me very strange
She said, "I think so, it was so long ago."

I said this is true, and I am glad to see you.
As I remembered her being shy.
Then I asked who, is this little guy?
This is Brian my son. As I greeted him our future had begun.
I got her number, and asked when, was a good time to call.
Little did we know we would talk all night after all?
That morning I had to be alert.   I had to go to work.
She was going to sleep, and I had a work load knee-deep.
All night we talked about our pass,
The last time we've seen each other last.
Now I can say that night she stole my heart.
Her values she held were smart.
She was sexy and sweet as she could be.
I couldn't believe this was happening to me.
Many times in life we don't understand.
The Impact, as life demands.
We can say in life what we will or won't do.
Only the Lord knows what will come true.
As I tell you this part, I can't tell you a lie
At this point, I was the bad guy
The story, as it was, is hard to believe
How is it we are so cold, and willing to deceive?
I now know what it means to be in the flesh
It took the spirit of the Lord to bring me through my mess
As it is said in the streets, men are dogs
Behold, this is nothing more than when his ego calls
Right is right and wrong is wrong
This is why some of us are all alone
We shared many good times as we fell in love
We were blessed by the Lord above
The road I was going down wasn't going to last
I was sinking in quicksand very fast
I prayed to Lord for insight
The desire of my heart was to set things right
To all that read this, I say to you,
"To yourself first be true.
Then your path in life will become clear to you."

To, come out of darkness, into the light
We must in our hearts desire to set things right
Things between us seemed to be lost
We didn't know how to recover and at what cost
The love of my life and I was at wits end
We humbled ourselves before Jehovah
Our life together now begins
I came close to losing the love of my life
Now the story has unfolded
My love, my life, my friend, and now, my wife

Inspiration Statement: Reflecting on my wedding day.

Our Wedding Day

The day has finally come to be
Many family and friends have come to see
On this day, we were blessed
Loved ones and friends wished us much success
It all started as the wedding party came through the door
Everything was so beautiful and couldn't be ignored
As, writer and groom, I stood
And watched everyone, enter the room
By my side, was my best-man
My new brother, I chose to make this stand
Joy and love, white doves
To share a day of grace and blessings from above
The many gifts and all the good food
Words can't express everyone's happy mood
A woman of the hour, a beautiful flower
To look at her you were wondering if she was rich and famous
Maybe she is a relative of the family Amos
We danced and we laughed
We talked about how we overcame our past
We overcame our fears
We discussed our problems, which fell on Jehovah's ears
Many people have tried to make relationships work
Some people have turned to their church
For some, that didn't work
For us, we desired to be as one
We agreed to let the Lord's will be done
We came to terms with our roles
Together, our story will unfold
We must keep our God in our circle, and in our loop
We went on with joy and tears,
All to be seen by family and peers
Our after-party was a time to remember
We made history the 29th day of September
That day, place, and time, was for me and this wife of mine

It came time for us to leave the scene
We took a ride in our limousine
The driver drove us around, and
We stopped to take pictures downtown.
She looked so beautiful by the waterfall
My heart had un-measurable joy, most of all
She was so lovely and awesome to see under the night lights
I'm proud to be her husband, blessed with a future so bright
We went on our honeymoon in a new car
To make our ship, we had to travel very far
We laughed and we rejoiced as we made our trip
Before we knew it, we arrive at Cape Canaveral
So we could board our cruise ship
The lines were long, but we didn't care
We were newlyweds in love and thankful to be there
As we walked in our room, she couldn't believe her eyes
My bride finally was able to see the many surprises
In our lifetime, we said we could not have dreamed
Of all we done and seen, what to us it truly means
Honeymoon of love, enjoying the best
Being out of the country and having no stress
We made many memories for the stories to be told
As we look through the windows
Of our eyes and what we behold
We arrived at the port about to end our trip
Kennedy Space Center launched a spaceship
We had a long drive before home could be reached
We came back by way of a Daytona Beach
To all that read this, we have shared this part of our life
As the writer and lyricist, it is important you know
How much I love my new lovely and beautiful wife

Inspiration Statement: Reflecting on my first year of marriage.

Our First Year

We traveled this first year, my role in it has become very clear
The year 2012, the 29th of September
A happy and loving day I will always remember
Today, there is only one clue
I'm speaking from the heart, that which is very dear and true
I can't begin to say how you make me have a loving day
It doesn't matter if work or play, you help me find my way
This lyric, my love, is just for you
You are the reason my heart stays true
Many things in life comes out of the blue
At times, if it wasn't for you, I may not have made it through
From the Lord, we are truly blessed
Through you, many days I'm free of stress
Mankind seeks to find a love like you, but you are all mine
It's plain to see how important you are to me
My lovely wife, you are the best
You free me from different stress
A lot of people go through life blind
Because of you, I can see love's truth
As I look through these eyes of mine
Through the course this first year
Many challenges of life appeared
Some people would have fear
Not me, as long as you were near
Your love I hold very dear and sincere
Our first year you have continued to
Show me how much I've been blessed
You bring me peace of mind, which allows me to rest
Good rest has much value
But the best for me is the fact that I have you
My love, with all you do
I want to say Happy Anniversary to you
And may our future hold many more
As the Lord opens the doors
For what He has in store

WISDOM

*"**Wisdom** is the most important thing..."*
–Proverbs 4:7

Inspiration Statement: Each day's challenges.

Today's Path

Every day, we desire to be content
Things we don't like make us give our two cents
As your day moves along
You always look for where you fit and belong
There are days that seem strange
Many days we go through seem to have no change
Many of us have a will to express how we feel
Are you ready to deal with people who seem not to keep it real?

With some, our anger gives us rage
How did we get to this stage?
To be a human, many times, carry burdens of the flesh
To reveal is to get a lot off of your chest.
Life's path road isn't easy
The wind blows at times breezy
There are many turns as you go
Your next stop, do you know?

Life's path, many times, will not be plain to see
Walk by faith and you will be able to find your destiny
Strive to have a pure heart
Others may never find it from the start
In life, we have to follow our own path
It's not a good thing for us to generate wrath
It's good and right to remain calm
Normally, this brings no harm
Seek to improve your everyday norm
When your path changes, you can weather the storm
As it comes in an evil form

It's important what you believe
Stay focused, so you won't be deceived
The price you pay can knock you to your knees
If you lost your way, take time to pray
Jesus is the way out of no way

Inspiration Statement: The key to life's clues.

The Key

The key is to reveal that which seems to be sealed
In everything we do, to apply the key finds out the reason why
The key to love is given by the living God above
We spend our life seeking a key to the right path
Many think it's something we cannot have
Life flows like running water from a valve

There's nothing new under the sun, when it's all said and done
Many say the key to learning makes you wise
Is this before or after we discovered life's lies?
Lies and deceit will always come from a mind that's weak
Never run from that which is true, this is a key clue
Life starts and stops with me and you

I wonder how many know what I mean
As you travel, just how much have you seen?
Every day of your life, there is a purpose for which you do
Some things are so simple, it's standing right next to you
Yes, that's right…it's a snake that bites
Can you focus on what's right?
Every day, you can find that it comes down to evil or good
Would you change it if you could?

The choice is yours…do you have your key to open the doors?
People say that life is very demanding
Behold, the key to life is wisdom, knowledge and understanding
I know, to many, this may seem strange
But be prepared to change
The key is to change, as life goes, there are many roles
As your story, unfolds
Don't be asleep, you must stay awake
You have much at stake
Open your eyes and don't be blind to the ways of Mankind

Remember this clue, and hold it true…this includes you too

Every day, the sun comes and then it's gone
Can you find your key on your own?
I hate to burst your bubble, to go alone is asking for trouble
Who, you may ask, to have with you along the way?
Jesus is with you each and every day

The Key

Inspiration Statement: To clear up the confusion of what love is.

Love Isn't

Love isn't when you beat me
Love isn't what you buy me
Love isn't when you hate me
Love isn't when you betrayed me
Love isn't when you lie to me
Love isn't where you take me
Love isn't money you gave me
Love isn't to let me have my way
Love isn't what you want me to say
Love isn't what you want me to do
Love isn't to control me
Love isn't to hurt me
Love isn't to desert me
Love isn't when I have to ask
Love isn't when you misuse me
Love isn't when you abused me

Love without the desire of righteousness
Will never become unconditional
Pure love is unconditional, with compassion of no end

Inspiration Statement: Every day's price.

A Price to Pay

In life, there is a price to pay every day
Today maybe a different day
But tomorrow will still have a price to pay
Some people may say, "You can have it your way."
Once or twice, in their minds, that's being nice

The price seems to give you what you want
Please take time to understand the do's and don'ts
Are you willing to sacrifice to obtain the things good in life?
To all, I will give you a valuable tip
There is a heavy price to pay for a good relationship

The price we pay for having our way
The price, the cost, is to know what we have lost
We ask ourselves, what brought it about?
Was it because we had many doubts?

The price we pay comes with many rules
Do you know what rule you may have abused?
"Get out, you have to go!"
These of some words people are quick to let you know

Some people say it is fate and karma
The bottom line yields it may, at times, be drama
The price can mean something we buy
Do you know why these things have caught your eye?

Don't doubt yourself or anyone
Truly isn't the way to get things done

Be careful what you seek, looking for a piece of mind
Jesus is the only one who can grant it to Mankind

To find joy and delight is to know when things are right
When things are looking up for you and your future looks bright

Then comes joy in the morning, oh, what a pretty sight!
If we have to pay a price, let it be good and not bad
Many times, the value makes us wish we never had

Inspiration Statement: A Mother's love.

Behold! The Story of Mother to Be Told

To be a Mother is to be like no other
From the day a child is born
Is the day a Mother is adorned
You can carry the weight of life
And you never think twice
Many people say, "I don't see how you do it."
That's because you make it look like there is nothing to it
Mother, you don't look for personal gain
All you want is to maintain
No matter how big a problem can be
Mother has a way of helping me see
I can be all I can be
No matter how the story is told
Mother, you have a heart of gold
It's not every now and then
She is a friend until the end
Friends may come and friends may go
Remember, Mother told you so
Mother, every day you pay the price
To ensure we have success in life
It's not hard to see
When you have a Mother that truly loves thee
Mother always say "It doesn't matter
Where a life you are bound,
Just make sure when you stand,
You stand on solid ground."
Mother, the essence of your love is never overdue
Because, every day, I feel the things you do
Your love is pure and true
Mother, from day to day, you seem to
Find a way out of no way
What the Bible says is true, next to God,
A Mother's love can see you through
All good gifts come from above
An example of that is a Mother's pure love
To be a Mother is like no other

Inspiration Statement: An insight of the time spent at work.

Time in the Workplace

As I start this, I say to you, I am only after that which is true
These words I say will pertain to everybody
The only Judge is God Almighty
To all who read, this is my style
I only want to tell the truth, and hold your attention for a while
Time in the workplace can leave a bitter or sweet taste
You must understand to work at a comfortable pace
During time in the workplace
You will see many things you don't like
You must let it go, and not hold on to haughtiness and spite
In the workplace, things are not always fair
The key is to always be aware
You can always say something about what people do
Pass judgment on the things that pertain to you
You have worked real hard and paid your dues
Yet and still, people think is okay for you to be misused
You seek ways to increase your odds
To be qualified and not denied
You have to fight the good old boy system, you see
In order to have a chance, to be all you can be
Time in the workplace, at times, build a team
On the other hand, in some places, it's only a dream
When you spend time in the workplace, you must hold the tool
You must know all the company's rules
Every day at work, you must choose the right path
If you choose the wrong one, you will feel the company's wrath
Time in the workplace, is a job that can bring you many friends
Then, there are enemies of no end
Some enemies you may know and some may hide
One thing is for sure, you will always seem to be tried
No matter what they might do, hold steadfast
Show the wisdom you have, with class
Soon, all the evil will pass
During time in the workplace, you have to hold your peace
Then, the Lord will make the chaos cease

For those of you that think you are in charge
You will never have teamwork when fairness is still at large
Time in the workplace requires managers
And leaders to be consistent
Or you will lose control in what seems to be an instant
You must not have favor and you must not waver
For it is and always will be proper behavior
So your desire is to lead?
Then you must be aware, at times, people have needs
The people must have faith in you
But they must know where you are leading them to
Don't tell them a lie, no matter how much you deny
You won't maintain if you're in it for personal gain
Time in the workplace, with people, is like one big team
That can overcome any thing, it seems
Time is spent worldwide
Millions of workers performed with pride
For we all must know our roles
In order to achieve company goals
Not just one or two, it will take all of us to see it through
For those of you that read this, and say these things are a lie
It is you that truth will deny

Time in the workplace

Inspiration Statement: The impact of leaving home.

To Have A Heart Will Travel

To all, far and near, please lend me your ear
For all the traveling you do, this one is for you
We never think when we leave home
How long we will be gone
As I write and it pertains to you
You have been blessed to know what is true
When we leave, we take all we've learned
We do it with no concern
We really don't know when we leave, all we need
Nor, do we know if we will do good deeds
Many times, we leave someone we love
Sometimes, we leave humble as a dove
Some of us leave seeking wisdom and knowledge
As we go off to college
Some of us leave in a bad way
And now sit in prison today
As we traveled, following our heart
It normally sets us apart
Don't dwell on the things you cannot change
But continue to show love
And people will say you are strange
Some of us leave to be the best we can be
It will only happen, if you let Jesus teach thee
You want to be the best
Jesus can teach you how to pass all of man's tests
Out of the heart flows the issue of life
Sometimes, issues will have us travel once or twice
Many of us may travel with spirit of mind
Even then, we must be kind
That which is Spirit, is spirit
That which is flesh, is flesh
We all must pass this test
Many people leave to be on their own
Soon to make camp in a town, calling it their new home
The same heart is still within

Of all the traveling you have done
How much was changing? Is it none?
When traveling to find a new city of our own
Old friends will say you are now gone
Have you seen him? Have you seen her?
This is the question many will ask
Soon they say, "I can't remember when I did last."
Many of us leave home for love, following a heart
Some soon find out, we shouldn't have from the start
Others find joy, love, peace, and success
Then only Jesus knows, what happened to the rest

Inspiration Statement: Compounding stress.

You're Too Blessed To Be Stressed

My sister, my brother, you are like no other
You're too blessed to be stressed
We will not settle for anything less, just because of stress
In all you do, please hold this thought close to you
You're too blessed to be stressed
We hold all the power, we can issue it every hour
It's yours to use because, in His Name, it's ours
When we pass the tests, Jesus removes all stress
We must understand, there is power in His Name
This is not a game, believe, and your life will not be the same
I am no holy roller, I put all my burdens on Jesus' shoulders
You don't have to cry
It's not for us to deny, all we have to do is try
Just hold your peace, Jesus will make the chaos cease
This is not a tease, in you, Jesus must be pleased
Don't walk around with a face looking mad
Don't hold a face looking very sad, rejoice and be glad!
He is not a toy, Jesus is the center of my joy
The one thing we should concern ourselves with most
Jesus is our heavenly host
It does not matter in life what we have to go through
There is only one thing you need to know to do
Call on the name of Jesus, and he will see you through
This I speak isn't a joke, many of us are unequally yoked
Some of us are being provoked
Many of us know the reasons why
We refuse to admit we are living a lie
We can't continue to deny
It's not just me, it's not just you
We all must know these things to be true
You're too blessed to be stressed
Many of us say Jesus was here and now He is gone
Remember this, Jesus has never left us alone
Some say you can talk until you're blue in the face
To help Mankind is just a waste

———

Words of Jesus, is more than just a taste
It's in the a.m., 3:21, time belongs to Jesus...He is the one
The bottom line is drawn by Him
He will say when things are done
You're too blessed to be stressed

Inspiration Statement: The emotional toll of being jobless.

Unemployed

Let's take time to explain how this condition sets us behind
A condition of this kind of affects a person's state of mind
How can we deal with this reality pill?
To feel as if your fate has been sealed
Many feel depressed because things develop into a big mess
To walk our path of life, we have to face what is real
For some of us, this can break our will
Unemployment's effects aren't exact
Everyone experiences a different impact
It's not strange to know many things would change
I must insist that everyone understand this is a long list

How did this happen?
Was it the good old boy system or was it just me?
Was it due to the economy? Can you really see?
How did this condition, come to be?
Like everyone else, including myself
To be unemployed consumes your wealth
Please hear me when I say this part
The lack of money creates a very big void
Leaving our state of mind annoyed
Do you have a little or a lot?
It can consume all you got
That's the money side
Stress from it can make your brain tired
All these years, I was the one to provide
Now applying for a job, I'm being denied
Let's keep it real, to cope with this is a big deal

As we talk to our God
People may say, what did you mumble?
No, I have been humbled
Many of us face court for child support
As we look for work, our driver's license has been suspended
How is that best for my child?

Is this what the court intended?
How can we be considered a dead beat
When at every turn, we are denied the work we seek?
Walk a day in my shoes and you will know what it feels like
To lose, be misused, and abused
Yes, in life, our direction is the way we choose
Yet, on the other hand, the world holds many fools
Who don't obey the rules of life's clues?
To save time, let's understand the bottom line

Every day, we have to deal with Mankind
As we try to stay in our lane and maintain, trying to stay sane
The evil doer is always there to gain
I am unemployed. What shall I do?
These bills have to be paid, too
Continue to do the best you can do
Never lose faith of what is just and true
Jesus is always there with you
As we do good deeds, He is aware of our needs
You can't hold a good man or woman down
As long as Jesus is around
Stay focused on what it takes to be heavenly bound
Your success will come back around

Inspiration Statement: A Father's love.

It Is Okay

It is okay to have emotions, and not be considered gay
It is okay for you to be humble and meek
And not be considered weak
It is okay for you to tell your wife and your kids
You love them and you wished him well
You shouldn't always raise hell

It is okay to find a job today
To feed your family without delay
It is okay when you are found to be wrong
Accept it and learn from it, then move on to be strong
It is okay to get rid of stubbornness and pride
Then, guilt has no place to hide

It is okay to practice what you preach
Then, you are qualified to teach
It is okay to trust in God as you travel through life
But make sure you know, if you trust Him, never think twice

It is okay to have goals in your life that you seek
Make sure you know all things are possible and can be reached
It is okay, as a man, you understand your role
This is very important in reaching your goals

So, to be a man and say, "It is okay."
For now, you have learned the true and just way

It is okay

Inspiration Statement: Being thankful for each day.

Another Day

Many of us often say, "Thank You, Lord for another day."
Let's take time to understand that line
The Lord will not have us blind
Another day has its appeal
We want to invoke our will
Another day isn't promised to the doubting Thomas
Each day, we must find our way
We must strive hard to see a living God

You may always want your way
What is the price you must pay?
We are mean and rude
And don't care if your brother has food
When you have found love
Can you learn to be humble as a dove?
My brother is holding hate
Can you be the one to set him straight?

The economy in life has gotten so very hard
We don't even know where to start
Mother and Father, it's not just up to you
Jesus is in this, too
On the job, many people have a lot to say
Some are right, some are wrong
How long has this problem been going on?

Satan will come at you in many ways
Only the strong will stand these days
On this day, I will say, "It's even harder to find my way."
Some days brings joy, some days seems to destroy
This is not a decoy, dealing with life isn't a ploy

For every morning you get your start
We must strive to be pure at heart
We must do what's right without delay

This is very important in finding our way
Another day is meant for all of you
And it's Jesus that helps you through
Challenges come and then they go
And when it's all over, do you really know?

For each day, this is our concern
From the challenges, have we learned?
It is said to practice what you preach
Then you know righteousness has been reached
When traveling life each day
Many of us lack the words to say
Each day seems to bring something different
That's only because the answers are not apparent

Each day holds many answers, if you know where to look
When the day is done, now you have learned what it took
Some of us grow old, some of us are wise
Behold the truth through Gods eyes
Man will try to justify everything he do
Did you consider, God can see that which is true
That which is spirit is spirit, and that which is flesh is flesh
Behold, this is one of life's greatest tests

To understand your spirit mind
Helps overcome tests of life over time
Desires of the flesh, has contributed to failure of many tests
Your flesh may be weak, but keep your spirit strong
Another day, just how far in life you've gone?
Is this clear to you?
Look through your eyes view
For each day you live, make sure that you are not living a lie
In the end, you will know the reasons why

Inspiration Statement: When things happen.

When

When analyzing, how tantalizing you are
A bright and morning Star
You have really raised the bar
Now it's known, a man must be up to par
As you go through and see all the envy and strife
You still must have a positive outlook on life
When the world beats you down and
Your desire is to be safe and sound
Remember, there is always someone around
To help you be heavenly bound
When you look beyond your needs, and still do good deeds
Then you know you have planted good seeds
When you know to do what's right is a must
Then you know in God you trust
When, as you travel place to place from day to day
Many will say they know the way
When it's your choice, to whom you can believe
Be careful not to be consumed and deceived
When you know life is about love and peace
Then and only then, will the chaos cease
When you know the world loves their own
Lines in life have been drawn
When it is clear the side you are on
Then you know you have grown
When you no longer let pride take you for a ride
Then guilt has no place to hide
When all of your goals seem as if they can't be reached
Then be humble and let it be known
In every thought, you can be taught
When it was a question we always ask
Really, we're not up to the task
The answer of "when" comes to pass
When travels of life puts you against all odds
And then is a good time to seek the Wisdom of God
So, the next time you say, "When?"
Now, you will know what to do then

Inspiration Statement: To challenge your knowledge.

Battle of the Minds

The battle of the mind is common among Mankind
Some of us try to force our will, as if there's this great appeal
Many say, "A mind is a terrible thing to waste."
It depends on each case, a little wisdom is only a little taste
There is always someone trying to match wits
There is wisdom and knowledge, and they don't know which

Many want to be players and many will hate
A true player knows what's at stake
As you look, you will find
They are a legend in their own mind
I say this to all, don't waste your time
My mind and your mind are two different things
We tend to forget that, it seems
One may win and one may lose
The path we take is what we choose
We first must know how we feel, to keep it real
To be bored can't be ignored
To be shy is to know the reason why
If you always want to hate
Then you need to get yourself straight
If you are broke, be wise and don't start selling coke
To truly live, is to know when it's time to give
To walk around always mad, is only because you are truly sad
Two rejoice at all times, is your choice
To be wise is when you are pleasing in God's eyes
To believe is to know you first must receive
To find relief, is to have a mind of peace
If you hold your peace, then Jesus will make the chaos cease
My body is tired, and my mind is weak
Then it is the strength in Jesus you seek
To always want to fight, does not make you right
To always sit and be alone is to know love is gone
If you hold to haughtiness and pride
Then, you have no solid guide
We say we want a battle of the mind
Are we really being smart at this time?

Inspiration Statement: Feeling alone in the world.

Alone

As we go through life, with all the chaos and strife
Being alone cuts like a knife
Many of us have a husband or wife
They don't always suffice

We want people around us that we feel care
With people, is like Russian roulette, a game of truth or dare
When we rolled the dice of life, we can't do some things twice

Being alone can bring so much pain
The burden is so heavy at times, relief is never gained
Many of us cry out, some sing and shout
This is what we need
In most cases, no one is willing to do good deeds

I am not trying to be witty, nor am I saying I want pity
Being alone sets a tone to figure out why all is gone
Did I contribute to this cause?
Am I the reason all is lost?
Now, I am paying the cost

Feeling alone is when our spirits seems to do well
For some of us, we say it's a living hell
Then, with others, we never can tell

Some of us try to hold a smile
But it only lasts for a little while
Others ask, "Is there a number I can dial?"
But the helpline we get makes us feel like a child

Many people don't know what to say
They don't know what I am going through today
I am looking to and fro for peace
This pain of being alone must cease
Being alone is spending time with self

This pain isn't meant for no one else

For many of us, being alone is something we choose to do
In those cases, I am not speaking to you
Some of you may say, "I am being an ass.
No, this problem we will handle with class."

Well, by now, you may be wondering what to do
I will give you a clue
First, know you can't lie to yourself
We cannot blame anyone else

For those of you that read this, please hear my cry
It is important to know the reasons why
Being alone sometimes can have a positive appeal
It's also the time to keep it real

Inspiration Statement: Forming the right relationships.

Relationships

This lyric today has many points to be made
I'm here to say what has been for many decades
Relationships can cover many and even a few
Today, I am going to focus on one or two

To start a relationship, someone has to catch our eye
One of the first things we will notice
Is whether they are bold are shy
Just as anything else, we must first understand ourselves

How can I be happy with you?
When I am not telling myself the truth?
In my mind, I must keep it real of how I feel
At all times, we must be willing to make the right choice.
When, in our spirit, we hear the little voice

We must be willing to love, live, and forgive
Truly, we all must know how these things feel
To yourself first be true
Then your path will become clear to you

Now, since we know how to start
When we walk this path, we can be smart
Relationships seem to always take a toll on the heart

In a relationship, we must know what type
In order to get it right
The type must not be blind to you
Otherwise, you will be lost and your direction will be, too

It's important to know this as we begin
If, in the beginning, we both feel we have a crush
It's very important to make sure it's not lust

We must, at all times, control our desire
Or our emotions and feelings will go haywire
To understand the difference between hate and love
Comes from the Lord above

Focus on your circle being close with a strong bond
Your friend with whom, you have fun
Keep the Lord in the middle
A lot, and not a little

If He is always there, He will keep you aware
Be aware and know, at all times, where you stand
This way, your relationship won't get out of hand
This applies to good friends, lovers, and any other

It can be a coworker or church member
That you have just met in December
Build all relationships on the truth and not a lie
So your future can build, live, and not die

When people say your name, you want them to have a smile
As we walk our path, it takes a while
We must build our relationships foundation on solid ground
At the same time, strive to be heavenly bound

Treat people how you want to be treated
If we don't, our relationship is already defeated
Everyday, relationships will undergo many tests
At times, it requires someone to confess

Don't point your fingers and say, "It wasn't me, it was you."
This isn't a good thing to do
First, start with the man in the mirror

Make things a little clearer

We must go into a relationship with focus and good intent
Not to have a place to vent
When all else fails, and things don't seem to be going well
Progress is hard to find and is hard to tell

Remember the best relationship you should have from the start
Is your relationship with a living God?
His Son's name is Jesus, and He is Jehovah
You must have a relationship with them before life is all over

Inspiration Statement: Reality.

Truth or a Lie

This lyric comes with many fears
Today is hard for a man to deal
With the reality of life as it appears
Many of us dread it, we know Jesus has said it

Our everyday path is impacted by truth or a lie
In ways I will now explain how and why
Your choices hold many consequences
When we choose wrong, it's hard to mend the fences

Let's take a moment to translate the many ways
Truth or lie is spoken of these days
True or false is used to answer paper tests
Mankind calls by request

Truth or dare is used to
Question whether you are aware
Left or right is to question your path to the light
Good or evil is to express your desire
And question what will be your retrieval?

Day or night is your choice, darkness or the light
Good or bad can bring happiness or sadness
The fast road for the slow, is to say
Think quickly and questions, do you really know?

High or low is to say, "Heaven or hell?"
And ask you to decide where you want to dwell
Up or down, life is like a roller coaster

Truth or a lie is an everyday choice
Relative to understand why we shouldn't deny
The reason our daily path is as it lies

Which way will you choose to go?

Do you know?
Where were you before?
What do you have at your core?
Will you continue to ignore what's in store?

Truth or lie, we must decide if we want to be
A green tree or one that is dry
Truth lies in our everyday path
As we look through the windows of our eyes

What would Jesus do?
What is His message to me and you?
Today, as we seek to find our way
Follow the path of things that are just and true

Jesus is located there and walks with you
Focus and keep your heart true

Inspiration Statement: Those difficult days.

When Life Gets Hard

This lyric is for all loved ones, family and friends
My heart also feels the burden
And pain this life brings
We work hard for our family
We want to do our part
Many of us are lost from the very start
Life, at times, can seem to beat us down
Every time we look around
To some, it seems we're doing good
To know the truth, many will say we're misunderstood
At all times, we must try to do our best
We must understand life is a big test
To hear this, many may say, "What do you mean?
You don't go through, nor have
You seen the things my life brings."
As a lyricist and a writer, I say this is true
Jesus knows all, and He is in me and you
Others say, "That's good and very nice,
But who are you to give me advice?"
As we travel life's path, we must understand the mixture
We must behold life's big picture
Take time to step outside the box, life has many roadblocks
Jehovah is The Key to all locks
It's important to know the difference between truth and lies
It's vital we understand how in life it applies
"To yourself, first be true.
Then your path in life will become clear to you."
To make it even more clear
We must start with the man in the mirror
To we recognize our life's role
Then, we can see our impact as life unfolds
What we do impacts more than me and you
The ripples are felt around the world, too
As Jesus said, "Father forgive them,
For they know not what they do."

We, as Mankind, must always focus
On that which is just and true
So, the next time you ask for the reason why
Someone could do something unrighteous and bold
It can be a simple lie that was told
Why would people do things like this?
We must understand what our path holds
Many twists, that imposes and insists
When times in your life gets hard
Remember, we have done all we can do
Jehovah has been in control from the start

Inspiration Statement: To share with you, the reader, who I am and how far I've come as a writer.

The Author

To many, I am the author
But, in my eyes, I am just another path-walker
We all have to walk in a path of life, many days are not so nice
People may see us and yet
They don't know where we have been
The fact remains, only the Lord knows where and when
I want to take time in this lyric to tell you who I am
Prophets of old had to sacrifice a Lamb
I am just like you today, going through many tests
Trials of life, not by request
My name is Zane Edwards, you may have heard
I am constantly seeking and learning God's Word
I am a simple, common man, searching the path of life
As I stand, in Jehovah's plan
I am nothing and He is All
Without Him, I continue to fall
Many things will happen to me and you
If we don't cling to that which is just and true
To learn more about me
Lyric's in this book allows you to see
The Lord has led me to write
I truly did not plan this, or have it in my sight
By trade, I am in Tool and Die
We can only guess where our future may lie
The Lord inspired me to do right
I continued by faith and not by sight
Jehovah has made it plain that there is power in His Name
No matter what comes against us as we go
I hold this in my heart to always know
As the Lord continues to give me insight and keep it real
I now understand that life is about His Will
All the lyrics in my book, I have truly lived
I have found all is relative to His Will
I have been blessed to have my own style
I hope and pray these messages are worthwhile

I just wanted to share insight as the Lord taught me
To share with each reader, assures me
We are of the same family tree
I feel blessed to be able to tell you this story
True insight is to know that no man gets God's glory
It's been a number of years since I started to write
To know now what the Lord has shown me, is a pure delight
The compassion of the Lord is something to see
He still allows me to be a part of His family tree
When your burdens are heavy and love seems to be lost
And you don't have what it takes to pay the costs
It gives you a peace of mind to know that Jesus is Boss
As you read, you may say, "What is this?"
The Lord is the Author, and there is no twist
I am the tool He chose to use, and bring you the Good News
My journey has been long and never straight
Many things I've done, I've learned to hate
Today now as I look back, I understand where I was at
Trials of life we must endure
Remember, Jesus always has the cure
The lyrics I have written, a special part
As I walk my path in life, they are joy to my heart
I say thank you to all that gives me credit
I do it with love and that will never edit
I will close with something valuable
You may have noticed I've learned
When I learned this, it was a big concern
To yourself first be true
Then, your path in life will become clear to you

The following section is reserved for you to express your thoughts and add notes to aid in your understanding of the lyrics in this book.

Notes

Notes

Notes

Notes

Notes

Notes

Notes

Notes

Notes

Zane Edwards offers dynamic Workshops, Lectures and Presentations designed to *Empower, Educate,* and *Uplift* **YOUNG MEN**. If you would like more information, or if you are interested in having Zane **SPEAK** at your event or organization, please use the contact information below:

Email: info@AuthorZaneEdwards.com

Phone: (470) 231-ZANE

Website: AuthorZaneEdwards.com

A Special Thanks From The Writer

I would like to acknowledge and thank the people who have influenced me as an author and writer. My lovely wife, Stephanie, helped shape the man I am today. She was there by my side when no one else would be. She saw beyond my faults and saw my needs. The pure love and support she gave me was priceless. The Lord truly blessed and shined on me when He gave her to me. If I am to be thought of as a great man, she is the great woman beside me who I love very much.

To my children: Jemeka, Jeremiah, Brian, and Joshua – you have shaped me as a Father and are my best friends. Thank you to my grandson Kailen and Daughter-in-law Sherie for bringing added joy to my life. Special thanks goes to my brothers Carey, Gregory, Andre, and a host of loved ones and friends who shared their cherished moments with me.

I would like to give a special thanks to my mentor and coach Tierica Berry at Affirmative Expression, LLC for being there to guide me in the path of completion in publishing this book. Also, many thanks to Hotep at Hustle University for a special and memorable training as an author and speaker. Thank you Mike "Kofi" Johnson at AMG Digital Media for designing an awesome book cover. Finally, a special thanks to my publisher Andre Jerry at Just Bee Cards, LLC for believing in my work.

As a gift to my readers, I'd like to give you an exclusive first read from my next project entitled:

"Self-Threat"

An excerpt from the forthcoming new book…

Man 2 Man: Life Lessons Mom Never Taught You

Self-Threat

This type of threat, many people haven't seen or even understand
What it means yet
This threat is complex and must not be taken out of context
You may say, "What's the big deal?"
This is an appeal, asking each reader to keep it real

Self-threat impacts us from our youth
The beginning stage is when we deny ourselves the truth
No matter how you and I may feel
Yet and still, self-threat is real

The meaning is to harm oneself and doesn't involve anyone else
Every day, as we try to find our way
Ask yourself, "Am I a threat to myself today?"

It must be your will to walk your path of life and
Understand your destiny must be fulfilled
We must avoid telling ourselves lies
This denies us understanding, where wisdom truly may lie

By and by, we must gain knowledge to understand
Why self-threat is the action we must deny
Denial by way of lies and deceit
Is the triple threat of defeat

Once we understand life rules
We can avoid being abused by seeking the tools
We must have because life can be cruel

Help yourself and don't depend on anyone else
Many of us are quick to say, "I am grown."
Do you really know how to be strong
Until you get where you belong?
Stand strong on your 2 feet and do not give into defeat
Stay focused and obtain the true and just path you seek

Being humble and meek, adjusting your position in life
Striving to be complete
Defeat comes when we lose sight
Of the path of truth we all should seek

Self-threat is not to know what to do next
Be of good cheer and have no fear
Control doubt as it appears

We are our worst enemy
Don't be a threat because you overreact
First, recognize where you are at
Your position, your status in life
Focus on the things that are good, righteous and nice

To focus on the bad things is the road of destruction
Many things turn out very bad
Then, we regret and wish we never had
Of all the things you must remember
Never forget to constantly say to yourself
*"I am **not** a self-threat."*

We hope you enjoyed this Just Bee Cards publication.
If you are interested in publishing your inspirational material, please
contact:

Just Bee Cards

2897 N. Druid Hills Road, Suite 296
Atlanta, GA 30329
(678) 870-4233
www.justbeecards.com

www.ingramcontent.com/pod-product-compliance
Lightning Source LLC
Chambersburg PA
CBHW052007090426
42741CB00008B/1594